TABLE OF CONTENTS

INTRODUCTION

A brief review of military literature from the past two decades reveals that many writers on military affairs have varying ideas about postmodern militaries and postmodern wars. One can discover that militaries may be considered postmodern if they operate in support of postmodern just war, they have transitioning organizations, they are science and technology centric, or because they simply are not modern anymore.[1] This research was conducted to better understand the shifting moral influences that underpin why and how nations fight, as well as to anticipate how these influences will play out as the era progresses. The term postmodernism applies because it captures the combination of the shifting sense of morality and the dramatic influence of technology.[2] Postmodern morality is both relative and personal, and these properties have implications for current beliefs about just war theory, which in turn, influences decisions related to why nations fight. This postmodern influence on international relations is characterized by empowering the marginalized and de-emphasizing state borders. Postmodernism is also technology and information centric, as reflected in modern weapons such as unmanned combat systems.[3] Considering all of these aspects of postmodernism together contributes to a larger understanding of potential shifts in the ways in which nations justify why and how they fight.

---

[1]C. Douzinas, "Postmodern Just Wars and the New World Order," *JOURNAL OF HUMAN RIGHTS* 5, no. 3 (2006). Charles C. Moskos and James Burk, "The Postmodern Military," in *The Military in New Times*, ed. James Burk (Boulder, CO: Westview Press, 1994), 146. Chris Hables Gray, *Postmodern War: The New Politics of Conflict* (New York: Guilford Press, 1997), 22 and 29. Each of these authors provides a different perspective on what constitutes postmodernism in the military.

[2]Gray, *Postmodern War: The New Politics of Conflict*, 29. Gray associates technology and information with postmodernism. There can be little doubt that the huge amounts of information available via technology influences perceptions of truth.

[3]The term "man" is used throughout this research as a generic term in it's traditional collective humanity denotation. It is not intended to reflect a bias toward the male gender or, more importantly, against the female gender.

The central idea advanced in this project is that the postmodern moral emphasis on humanitarian intervention, when combined with the postmodern means of unmanned combat vehicles, portend a shift in the international system toward an international police organization with the authority and means to execute police functions within otherwise sovereign states. Explaining and understanding this thesis requires knowledge of postmodern morals and how they have gained influence in international relations. It also requires an understanding of the postmodern means of warfare and how the employment of unmanned combat vehicles stands in the light of just war theory—are they a just means of combat? These conclusions in this thesis, both explicit and implicit, are important for military planners to understand if they are to be effective planners, advisors and leaders. They provide insight into the strategic context in which militaries operate, as well as the potential implications of military plans in execution.

Also, the moral component of this research is of particular importance. The military educational system typically limits ethics training to brief discussions of military ethical dilemmas or the Geneva Conventions. However, there is great value for the military planner to have a basic understanding of moral philosophy as it stands today, as well as its historical development, and how these influences are manifested in the international arena. The moral elements weaved throughout this research will create this general understanding.

This study is significant because it links the increasingly prevalent postmodern moral ideas about the use of international violence with the postmodern means of drone warfare to determine their significance. International laws and norms must be able to justify when the use of violence is appropriate, and bound the permissible means of violence, if it is to remain a legitimate construct for maintaining order among nations. But the postmodern moral ideas that result in pressures to utilize military force for humanitarian intervention, as well as the postmodern means of unmanned combat systems strain the current system. Thus, as these reasons for war and the means of war shift, international laws and norms must adapt. Therefore, as this

2

thesis contends, the use of unmanned combat systems in humanitarian intervention portends a change in the role of international bodies to meet these new demands.

To avoid confusion in the progress of the argument, the definitions of both humanitarian intervention and unmanned combat vehicles must be specified up-front. First, humanitarian intervention is distinguished from other forms of intervention based on the intervening nation's intent. For instance, NATO's intervention in Kosovo was justified on humanitarian grounds—to protect the Kosovars from mass atrocity at the hands of the Serbs. This differs from, for example, the Chinese intervention in the Korean War, which was a political decision for national interests. The distinction between the two types of intervention is important because they have different implications within the international system.

Also necessary is a distinction between *unmanned combat systems* and unmanned systems or other long-range weapon systems. Two criteria are required for a weapon system to fall into the category of unmanned combat system as used below. First, the weapon system must be directly involved in combat operations—specifically, the killing of perceived enemy combatants. This distinguishes unmanned combat systems from other unmanned systems, such as those that collect intelligence or detect and destroy improvised explosive devices. A second characteristic of unmanned combat vehicles is that they permit the operator to reside in a sanctuary outside of the battlefield to operate the system as a technological extension of human agency. This distinguishes unmanned combat systems from other long-range weapon systems such as ballistic missiles or cruise missiles. Such a distinction is important because a common defense for the employment of unmanned combat systems is that they are similar in effect to cruise or ballistic missiles, only with more precision, and because this distinction also excludes autonomous systems. Fully autonomous systems are not considered here because they completely remove moral decision-making from the battlefield environment in both time and space since they operate as a result of prior programming. Whereas unmanned combat systems only separate

3

the moral agent from the battlefield in space. Autonomy adds a separate level of complexity that is unnecessary for the conclusions drawn herein.

This research is qualitative and utilizes primary and secondary sources that are multi-disciplinary, including philosophy, international politics, and law. It begins with a brief history of the moral foundations of the just war tradition to demonstrate how this foundation has shifted with time, as well as its subsequent influence on international law. This will establish the moral context for understanding the debate surrounding humanitarian intervention taken up in the following section. The results of the research into the debate regarding humanitarian interventions show a recent shift in how nations justify these types of operations, as well as the need for an international authority to approve them. Finally, the discussion closes by considering the impact of unmanned combat systems on both moral considerations in the combat environment as well as the moral viability of such a means to achieve the ends of humanitarian interventions. The conclusion will synthesize the previous three sections and show how they presage an international police organization with the authority and means to execute police functions within otherwise sovereign states.

The moral debate regarding the use of current unmanned combat systems is still nascent because their first use in targeted strikes was only a decade ago and because the populace at large has only become aware of such activities in the last few years.[4] The debate regarding humanitarian intervention, on the other hand, began shortly after the Cold War as U.S. troops deployed for humanitarian missions to various parts of the globe. So the latter is more developed. Yet before delving into such topics, it is important to understand the moral philosophy that informs both debates.

---

[4]Bill Yenne, *Attack of the Drones: A History of Unmanned Aerial Combat* (St. Paul, MN: MBI Pub. Co., 2004), 8-9. Yenne tells the story of the first targeted shooting from an unmanned aerial platform, which occurred November 4, 2002 in Yemen.

POSTMODERN MORALS: EXALTING THE MARGINALIZED, OPPOSING POWER STRUCTURES

Views on the morality of war can range from the one extreme that all war is immoral, to the opposite extreme that moral principles do not apply. For the purposes of this research, it is assumed that moral values outlined in the just war tradition are vital for providing the language for assessing the justice of the decision to resort to war, *jus ad bellum*, as well as the justice of the actions in war, *jus in bello*.[5] As Clausewitz ardently stressed, "Military activity is never directed against material force alone; it is always aimed simultaneously at the moral forces which give it life, and the two cannot be separated."[6] To take the life of another human is obviously an act of moral significance, evidenced by the fact that such actions must be justified. The just war tradition provides the language to make such determinations. If a combatant fights by the rules, he avoids the moral guilt that killing would otherwise require. Additionally, a nation can also avoid the guilt of charging its combatants to kill if it can justify its decision to go to war under the just war tradition. Many of the individual principles within the tradition are not codified in international law, yet they are generally accepted as common international practice. This is similar to how some principles of individual morality are codified into law, and some are not.[7] Additionally, as a tradition, the just war theory has a history, and as a moral system, it has a foundation that gives it authority. Understanding the moral foundations of the just war tradition,

---

[5]The topic of moral values can be contentious. For the purposes of this research, the term "moral values" refers to the principles of the just war tradition, specifically in their utility in determining the moral acceptability of war related decisions.

[6]Carl von Clausewitz, *On War*, trans., Michael Howard and Peter Paret (Princeton, NJ: Princeton University Press, 1976), 137. Clausewitz's views of moral values in relation to war are generally personal, rather than collective, and relate more to human agency and will than to moral ought.

[7]The Geneva Conventions deal primarily with the principles of *jus in bello*, and the U.N. charter addresses *jus ad bellum*. The traditional principles associated with *jus ad bellum* are not addressed directly in the U.N. charter, rather the U.N. Security Council under Article VII is the body charged with determining if the use of force is appropriate internationally.

and more importantly, how it has shifted over the centuries, is relevant to this research because during the early seventeenth century the tradition was systematized to become the basis for the international order that exists today. Also, it provides the context from which to understand postmodern moral views.

This section will provide a brief history of moral philosophy and its implications for the just war tradition to provide context for how Western ideas regarding the foundations of moral systems have shifted over time. This will permit understanding postmodern morality as it contrasts with its historical predecessors—the classical and the modern views—to demonstrate why postmodern morality exalts the marginalized and opposes power structures.

Prelude to Postmodernism: A Brief History of Classic and Modern Moral Philosophy and the Just War Tradition

It is necessary at this point to review the history of moral philosophy over the last two millennia to understand the basis for moral reasoning that existed prior to postmodernism. This history fits into two broad categories based on the philosophical foundations of knowledge during the era. First is the classical era, which spans from the time of Constantine until the Age of Enlightenment, or from the early fourth century to the mid seventeenth. In this era, knowledge was authoritative based on its appeal to God and revelation. The modern era, which follows the classic era, runs from the Enlightenment until the mid to latter decades of the twentieth century. This is when the authority required to claim knowledge shifted away from the divine, toward reason and empirical verification. The postmodern era, which began around the middle of the twentieth century, involved a further shifting of moral foundations, which will be addressed subsequently.[8] Thinkers as far back as the early classic era still influence current thoughts on international issues, from sovereignty to just war, and this era is where the study begins.

---

[8]These delineations are common in historical literature. Rather than justify them here, the

Classic Era Moral Philosophy and Just War Theory

The classic era in the West was dominated by Christian influences. After the conversion of Constantine in the early fourth century, Christianity became the official religion of the Roman Empire. In the Judeo-Christian tradition, God created man in his own image and provided him the means to distinguish good from evil. Thus, the Judeo-Christian God served not only as the objective foundation for defining knowledge and morality, he was also the ultimate executor of justice on those who would persist in violation of his principles. This intellectual tradition runs from Augustine through Aquinas and up to the early modern authors such as Hugo Grotius and Francisco de Vitoria.

Howard Hensel, professor of political and military affairs at the United States Air War College and editor of several books on the subject of just war, referred to classic era moral philosophy in terms of theocentric natural law.[9] The adjective "theocentric" denotes a foundation in the divine. Also, natural law, in the words of scholastic era theologian Saint Thomas Aquinas, is a body of self-evident truths, of which the first principle is "good is to be sought and evil avoided."[10] All other principles, said Aquinas, are based on this one.[11] In a sense, natural law is what delineates good and evil, and humans have an inherent ability—reason—to perceive it.[12]

---

necessity for these distinctions between eras will become evident throughout the section. Also, it is important to note that each era only introduced a new basis or understanding of knowledge and did not fully supersede previous beliefs. Each tradition retains some level of influence in subsequent thought. In short, there are still thinkers that understand knowledge in the classical and modern sense today even though this is the postmodern era.

[9]Howard M. Hensel, "Anthropocentric Natural Law and Its Implications for International Relations and Armed Conflict," in *The Legitimate Use of Military Force: The Just War Tradition and the Customary Law of Armed Conflict*, ed. Howard M. Hensel (Aldershot, England: Ashgate, 2008), 5-27.

[10]Thomas Aquinas, *Summa Theologica* (1274), Question 94, Article 2.

[11]Ibid.

[12]This definition of natural law coheres perfectly with common conceptions of morality.

Given this, Hensel defined theocentric natural law as divinely inspired standards that shape and evaluate both individual and collective behavior.[13] Hensel identified seven components of this view of natural law, two of which are particularly relevant for this discussion. First, Hensel concluded that theocentric natural law is higher law, which is above the pressures of community and the customs and laws common to all people.[14] He also concluded that all people owe allegiance to this higher law.[15] Thus, the classical, God-centered view of morality provided warrant to view all mankind as accountable to a single moral code. This is the context in which the Western views of just war theory first developed.

The classical views of the early Christian church served as the foundations of the Western just war tradition, particularly in the writings of St. Augustine.[16] Part of his purpose in writing was to provide a moral foundation for Christians to take up arms in defense of the Roman Empire. In this effort, St. Augustine primarily covered the reasons for Christians to go to war. What he explicated influenced the *jus ad bellum* subcategory of the just war tradition. Centuries later, the great Middle Ages scholar and theologian Saint Thomas Aquinas, in *Summa Theologica*, expressed more clearly the requirements that encompass *jus ad bellum*.[17] Aquinas defined the just reasons for resort to war beyond the current ideas of defending the common well

---

The two can be thought of as one and the same throughout this paper.

[13]Howard M. Hensel, "Theocentric Natural Law and the Norms of the Global Community," in *Sovereignty and the Global Community: The Quest for Order in the International System*, ed. Howard M. Hensel (Aldershot, Hants, England: Ashgate, 2004), 1.

[14]Hensel, "Theocentric Natural Law and Just War Doctrine," 8.

[15]Ibid.

[16]However, St Augustine was not the first to write about the just causes of war. For a review of other just war traditions see Paul Robinson, *Just War in Comparative Perspective* (Aldershot, Hampshire, England: Ashgate, 2003).

[17]Aquinas, *Summa Theologica*, Second Part of Book 2, Question 40. Aquinas cites both Augustine and the Bible in his explication of just war doctrine.

being against external threats. He offered in addition that sovereign states might justify war to secure peace, punish evildoers, and uplift the good.[18] The highly respected historian of just war James Turner Johnson contended that, based on this rendering of sovereign responsibility, the classic view of sovereignty included the responsibility to ensure a just order among states.[19] Just as individuals retain their rights as long as they act justly, so too sovereign states retain their rights as long as they act justly. However, if they do not, under the classic view, other sovereign authorities have the right, maybe even responsibility to ensure justice.

There are two key takeaways from this survey of the classical view of natural law that are relevant for the follow-on reasoning. The first is that God provides coherence to the entirety of the moral system. As a single authority whose nature defined good, and thereby evil, God's standard was the measure for *all* behavior, for *all* humans, for *all* time. Secondly, the rights of the individual, as well as those of the sovereign, both depend on their adherence to God's law. Within this single system of values, individuals and nations can prioritize rights and responsibilities. However, this rendering of moral values and duties met a substantial challenge in the sixteenth century. The challenge to the authority of the Catholic Church by the Protestants marked the beginning of the transition to the modern era.

Modern Era Moral Philosophy and the Systemization of Just War

Beginning around the time of the Reformation and the wars between Protestant nations and Catholic nations, the classical view of morality in the West began a dramatic shift. Aided partly by the success of the natural sciences, the authority for knowledge in both philosophy and science was viewed by many Enlightenment era thinkers to be man's ability to reason, and God

---

[18]Ibid., Quesiton 40, Article 1.

[19]James Turner Johnson, *Ethics and the Use of Force* (Burlington, VT: Ashgate, 2011), 50.

was rendered unnecessary.[20] Among the earliest was Thomas Hobbes, who believed that there is

no ultimate good or greatest aim, but "the object of man's desire, is not to enjoy once only, and

for one instant of time; but to assure for ever, the way of his future desire."[21] According to

Hensel, the movement away from theocentric natural law left a void that required a "new,

authoritative ultimate source of law," to which there were two responses.[22] The first is what

Hensel described as the anthropocentric view of natural law. This view is characterized by

independence from divine or ecclesiastical authority, in which all knowledge depended on human

reason.[23] Natural law remained, but it was independent of any authority. This view is represented,

according to Hensel, by two camps—Hobbesian realists or Lockean liberals.[24] Then, by the end

of the Enlightenment era, natural law was rejected altogether. This second response obviated the

need for authority to justify natural law. Hensel represented this era by reference to several

authors including Hegel and Clausewitz.[25] For both of these groups, the foundations for moral

beliefs were relative to what one believed was mankind's motivation. As Hensel contended, from

---

[20]Hensel, "Anthropocentric Natural Law and Its Implications for International Relations and Armed Conflict," 30. For a macro view of Western civilization from the Greeks to modern day as reflected in philosophy, science, art and religion see Francis Schaeffer, *How Should We Then Live? (L'abri 50th Anniversary Edition): The Rise and Decline of Western Thought and Culture* (Wheaton, IL: Crossway Books, 2005). See also Nancy Pearcey, *Saving Leonardo: A Call to Resist the Secular Assault on Mind, Morals, & Meaning* (Nashville, TN: B&H Publishing, 2010).

[21]Thomas Hobbes, "Leviathan," (1651), Chapter XI. Quoted from the Kindle Edition.

[22]Hensel, "The Rejection of Natural Law and Its Implications for International Relations and Armed Conflict," 88.

[23]Hensel, "Anthropocentric Natural Law and Its Implications for International Relations and Armed Conflict," 30.

[24]Ibid.

[25]Hensel, "The Rejection of Natural Law and Its Implications for International Relations and Armed Conflict."

the perspective of anthropocentric natural law "all morality is subjective and situational."[26] These moral views are also evident in modern era just war thinkers.

In 1625 the Dutch jurist, Hugo Grotius published *De Jure Belli ac Pacis Libri Tres*.[27] Many know Grotius as the father of international law because of this work.[28] Grotius clearly wrote from a classical perspective, frequently using God as an authority. However, one purpose of his work was to elucidate a systematized form of international rules, whether based on natural law, divine ordinance or custom.[29] He wanted to create a system that would be relevant in an international context in which not all states recognized Christianity or the Christian God. Therefore, while Grotius honored God as the author of natural law, he constructed his system in a way that made God tertiary and replaceable.[30] In his rendering of just war, Grotius simultaneously removed the tradition from its foundation, and emphasized the sovereign over the humanitarian concerns.

The evidence that Grotius simultaneously honored God, while rendering him unnecessary to the application of international order, is in the way he defined natural law,

---

[26]Hensel, "Anthropocentric Natural Law and Its Implications for International Relations and Armed Conflict," 54.

[27] Translated, *On the Law of War and Peace: Three Books*

[28]Hamilton Vreeland, *Hugo Grotius, the Father of the Modern Science of International Law* (New York: Oxford University Press, American Branch, 1917). Christoph A. Stumpf, *The Grotian Theology of International Law: Hugo Grotius and the Moral Foundations of International Relations*, ed. Gustavo Benavides and Kocku von Stuckrad, Religion and Society, vol. 44 (Berlin: Walter de Gruyter, 2006), 4.

[29]Hugo Grotius, *De Jure Belli Ac Pacis Libre Tres*, ed. James B. Scott, trans., Francis W. Kelsey, Classics of International Law, vol. 2 (New York: Oceana Publications, 1964), 9.

[30]Phillip Wesley Gray, "'That Truth That Lives Unchangeably': The Role of Ontology in the Just War Tradition," (College Station, TX: Texas A&M University, 2007). http://hdl.handle.net/1969.1/4715. Gray explores the evacuation of Augustinian ontological thought from the just war tradition.

> The law of nature is a dictate of right reason, which points out that an act, according as it is or is not in conformity with rational nature, has in it a quality of moral baseness or moral necessity; and that, in consequence, such an act is either forbidden or enjoined by the author of nature, God.[31]

Note how Grotius used the phrase "author of nature," then placed "God" after a comma as an addendum to the definition. This added only a personal touch to his definition—it remained fully functional and retained all of its meaning without this suffix, and clearly emphasized reason and rationality as central to natural law. Christoph A. Stumpf, professor of law at Martin Luther University in Germany, in his detailed study of Grotius's theology concluded that Grotius viewed the state as only a human establishment and that the governed are not allowed to resist injustices inflicted on them by the sovereign.[32] According to James Turner Johnson, this view of sovereignty was codified in a sense, in the Westphalian order that also defined sovereignty, not in terms of responsibility, but in terms of *de facto* rule.[33]

Stumpf further argued that, even though Grotius's beliefs were in line with Christian tradition, his approach was compatible with modern liberal theories of international law, which "neither contend nor refute any religious positions."[34] Grotius's systematized construct for international law in general, as well as his rendering of just war theory in particular, permitted a secularized form of the moral code determined by reason. This construct was the foundation of the international order that is in place today, and was a major influence on modern perceptions of the just war tradition.

---

[31]Grotius, *De Jure Belli Ac Pacis Libre Tres*, 38-9 [Grotius, Book I. Chap. I. X.I.].

[32]Stumpf, *The Grotian Theology of International Law: Hugo Grotius and the Moral Foundations of International Relations*, 153-4.

[33]Johnson, *Ethics and the Use of Force*, 51.

[34]Stumpf, *The Grotian Theology of International Law: Hugo Grotius and the Moral Foundations of International Relations*, 36.

Before Grotius, there was a direct connection between the just war tradition and its moral foundation, God. After Grotius, the moral foundation of just war was relative to the national belief system. Therefore, the just war foundation could only be as objective as the moral system that served as its foundation. This made it inherently relative and refutable across cultures, since it could no longer be justified objectively. Therefore, even contemporary discussions commonly neglect or mishandle the topic of moral bases, either intentionally or not.

Michael Walzer penned the baseline work that invigorated the most recent discussion of just war theory with his highly influential 1977 book, *Just and Unjust War*. Nearly every major article or book on the topic cites Walzer's work. Yet, early in his book, Walzer stated, "I am not going to expound morality from the ground up. Were I to begin with the foundations, I would probably never get beyond them; in any case, I am by no means sure what the foundations are."[35] That he pled agnosticism on the topic is not problematic for his argument given that he reasoned from existing international law. More recently, David Fischer, senior fellow at King's College in London, recognized this deficiency in the contemporary just war construct in his book *Morality and War*. He said that one of the challenges to the tradition is that it has become detached from "ecclesiastical authority or any wider philosophical or theological underpinning."[36] Fischer resurrected the Aristotelian emphasis on virtues and offered "virtuous consequentialism" as a philosophical underpinning to resolve this problem.[37] However, the rational basis he provided does not re-attach the system to any objective foundation. His system is normative and of most value to those who desire rationality and emphasis on virtues as a moral guide. Both of these

---

[35]Michael Walzer, *Just and Unjust Wars: A Moral Argument with Historical Illustrations* (New York: Basic Books, 1977), xx.

[36]David Fisher, *Morality and War: Can War Be Just in the Twenty-First Century?* (Oxford; New York: Oxford University Press, 2011), 2.

[37]Ibid., 134-148.

highly respected commentators on the just war tradition demonstrate the challenge of discussing the morality of war, particularly the moral foundations for just war, in a secular context.

The classical views of morality provided the foundations and principles that originally shaped the Western just war tradition, and in the modern era they were systematized and removed from their foundation. The secularization and subsequent rejection of natural law during the modern era has had two lasting effects on how the just war tradition came to be viewed throughout the modern era. In contrast to the conclusions drawn from the survey of classical moral views, the modern era foundational shift to a secularized version of construct rendered it relative and applicable only to those nations that accepted its principles.

This brief rendering of the classic era and modern era moral foundations and the influence each perspective had on the just war tradition sets the context for current understandings of postmodern morality. Understanding how postmodern moral views developed, as well as what they value, is essential to recognizing their influence on what constitutes postmodern just war.

Postmodern Morality: Relative and Opposed to Power Structures

The mid twentieth century generally marks the beginning of the transition to the postmodern era. Philosophers who accept the title "postmodern" generally view knowledge and authority in terms of narratives and metanarratives that exist in order to gain and retain power.[38] To understand morality in the postmodern context, it helps to understand the broader reasons for the transition from the modern era to the postmodern era. Theologian and historian, David Wells, discussed this transition and noted that the optimism in the Enlightenment belief that meaning and morality could be discovered "within the bounds of natural reason and without reference to God"

---

[38]Jean-Francois Lyotard, *The Postmodern Condition: A Report on Knowledge* (Minneapolis: University of Minnesota Press, 1984), xxiii-xxv.

was destroyed by the horrendous events of the twentieth century.[39] Further, Wells wrote that the Enlightenment belief that "knowledge is always good, that knowledge is salvific, is mocked by our deep fears regarding scientific and technological accomplishments, many of which can as easily be used to thwart human well-being as to promote it."[40] The French postmodern philosopher Jean-Francois Lyotard, who is generally credited with applying the term "postmodern" to the era, corroborates Wells' synopsis,

> The nineteenth and twentieth centuries have given us as much terror as we can take. We have paid a high enough price for the nostalgia of the whole and the one... We can hear the mutterings of the desire for a return to terror, for the realization of the fantasy to seize reality. The answer is: Let us wage war on totality.[41]

The postmodern response was to reject modern natural law, as well as objective rules and boundaries in general. Wells noted, "any number of schemes of justice and forms of rationality now serve as warrants for a multitude of beliefs and practices; there is no longer any firm consensus as to what constitutes an absolute."[42] This lack of absolutes has clear implications for postmodern morality. Since the dialogue is open to "any number of schemes," the scheme adopted by the postmodern ethicist is less about right and wrong, and more about knowledge and power.

Suzan Ilcan, a professor of sociology and legal studies at the University of Waterloo in Canada, wrote on the subject in her introduction to the book *Postmodernism and the Ethical Subject*. She stated that the postmodern ethical studies contained in the book are a "departure

---

[39]David F. Wells, *God in the Wasteland: The Reality of Truth in a World of Fading Dreams* (Grand Rapids, MI: W.B. Eerdmans, 1994), 46.

[40]Ibid.

[41]Lyotard, *The Postmodern Condition: A Report on Knowledge*, 81-2.

[42]Wells, *God in the Wasteland: The Reality of Truth in a World of Fading Dreams*, 219.

from the imposition of modern/colonial moralities and their efforts towards the 'reduction of pluralism,' the devaluation of multiple subjectivities, minority positions, and competing knowledges."[43] Her contention was that postmodern ethics are situated in "fluid, life-enhancing encounters rather than in transcendent moralities that dictate what is dutiful."[44] The postmodern scheme of morality is not about imposing individual perceptions of right and wrong on social interactions. Rather, it "offers an implicit critique of the reign of Western objectivity and domination."[45] A postmodernist, according to Ilcan, "seeks to open the fractured or dislocated nature of totalities, explore the fluidity of boundaries and identities, and expose the potential for differences within situated knowledge."[46] This includes moral knowledge, which defines the boundaries of right and wrong in common human interaction.

Reasoning from the postmodern view, there are no absolutes, and there are no objective moral truths—all morality is relative and a matter of perspective. This includes the just war tradition, which has brought some criticism. David Fischer wrote that since the postmodern relativist's position has no objective basis for morality, then all ethical judgments are equally valid or invalid; therefore, there are no grounds to condemn Stalin, Hitler or any mass killing of innocents.[47] This argument is true of any moral system that does not have an objective basis. However, the postmodern emphasis is not on truth, rather it is on narrative, particularly the

---

[43]Suzan Ilcan, "From Modernity to Postmodernity," in *Postmodernism and the Ethical Subject*, ed. Barbara Gabriel and Suzan Ilcan (Montreal, QC, CAN: McGill-Queen's University Press, 2004), 27.

[44]Ibid., 28.

[45]Ibid., 26.

[46]Ibid., 26-7.

[47]Fisher, *Morality and War: Can War Be Just in the Twenty-First Century?*, 41.

narratives with a genesis outside of power structures. This explains the postmodern exaltation of the oppressed narratives, and antipathy toward power structures.

Lyotard's exhortation to "wage war on totalities", and Ilcan's emphasis on minority positions characterize the purpose of postmodern thought—to deconstruct power structures by undermining their narratives in the exaltation of oppressed narratives. With these ideas as a foundation, the only discernable principle within postmodern morality is a negative one best characterized as anti-domination. In the international arena, states are the power structures that warrant deconstruction by magnifying competing narratives. This has the laudable practical effect of emphasizing humanitarian concerns among the world's oppressed peoples. The implications of this will be drawn out in the next section.

To summarize the three views of morality, the classical view holds that God is the foundation of morality, and thereby, all mankind are accountable to his code. This was the context in which the just war tradition was founded. During the modern era, however, God and revelation was removed as a basis for knowledge, including moral knowledge. The just war tradition, as systematized by Grotius, reflects this foundational change. The postmodern transition contended that all claims of knowledge are attempts to attain power, and countered the narratives of the existing power structures by exalting the narratives of the marginalized. This postmodern view of morality explains, at least in part, the international acceptance of humanitarian intervention. But to understand the debate that surrounds humanitarian intervention, it is necessary to view it through each of the moral lenses surveyed above.

POSTMODERN ENDS: HUMANITARIAN INTERVENTION

The UN Charter, drafted and signed in 1945, valued national sovereignty over human rights.[48] The Soviets were one of the states to most ardently resist stronger language supporting humanitarian concerns. They reasoned that strong emphasis on the primacy of national sovereignty in the international order was the best way to advance socialism.[49] Still, the U.N. Charter addressed human rights in stating that the organization shall promote, "universal respect for, and observance of human rights and fundamental freedoms for all."[50] Also, in parallel discussions, the Geneva conventions and the efforts of the International Committee of the Red Cross kept humanitarian concerns on the international docket.[51] The primary friction in the current debate regarding humanitarian intervention involves the relative value of human rights and state sovereignty.[52] Both elements have normative moral justifications. State sovereignty is generally understood as either a right to rule or as a responsibility to citizens. Humanitarian intervention is understood in the sense of shared responsibility for the protection of human dignity. Therefore, the core issue in the debate has centered on which of the two values should have priority. A growing international consensus in the decades since the end of the Cold War has been that with sovereignty comes the responsibility to protect fundamental human rights.

---

[48]For background on the genesis of the U.N. charter see Geoffrey Best, *War and Law since 1945* (Oxford: Oxford University Press, 1994), 75-9. See also Susan E. Rice and Andrew J. Loomis, "The Evolution of Humanitarian Intervention and the Responsibility to Protect," in *Beyond Preemption: Force and Legitimacy in a Changing World*, ed. Ivo H. Daalder (Washington, D.C.: Brookings Institution Press, 2007), 59-60.

[49]Best, *War and Law since 1945*, 78.

[50]*Charter of the United Nations and Statute of the International Court of Justice*, (San Francisco: 1945), Chapter 9, Article 55.

[51]Best, *War and Law since 1945*, 79.

[52]For brief descriptions of the debate see International Commission on Intervention and State Sovereignty, *The Responsibility to Protect* (Ottawa: International development research centre, 2001), 2. See also Hensel, "Theocentric Natural Law and the Norms of the Global Community," 39-43.

Specifically, sovereign nations ought to intervene in the internal affairs of other states to protect innocent civilians from mass atrocities such as genocide. In fact, today's theorists almost universally allow for the moral permissibility of humanitarian intervention under certain conditions.[53] It seems as though the principle of non-intervention espoused by John Stuart Mill, and more recently by Samuel Huntington, is all but silenced in the current public discourse.[54] Thus the debate has become less about whether or not to intervene, and more about when and how.

Since armed humanitarian intervention involves the assumption of risk, its growing acceptance creates additional moral questions. Which nation should assume risk? Can a state rightly require its military members to assume personal risk for the sake of civilians from another state, to whom they have no sworn obligation? This section will present the moral arguments involved in the humanitarian intervention debate from each of the moral perspectives provided above. The conclusion will show that the postmodern moral influence is increasing the priority for humanitarian intervention without a concomitant emphasis on sovereignty. This is driving the authority for justice in the international system away from the state and toward the international system itself.

The Classical View of Humanitarian Intervention

In the classical view of natural law and international relations, as has become apparent, states derive their sovereign authority from God, and executing justice for the community is a

---

[53]David Lefkowitz, "On a Duty of Humanitarian Intervention," in *New Wars and New Soldiers: Military Ethics in the Contemporary World*, ed. Paolo Tripodi and Jessica Wolfendale (Farnham Surrey, UK: Ashgate, 2011), 87.

[54]John Stuart Mill, "A Few Words on Non-Intervention," *Foreign Policy Perspectives*, (London: Libertarian Alliance, 1859). Michael Walzer's discussion of J.S. Mill's non-intervention views in Walzer, *Just and Unjust Wars: A Moral Argument with Historical Illustrations*, 87ff. For Huntington's argument see, Samuel P. Huntington, "New Contingencies, Old Roles," *Joint Forces Quarterly*, no. 34 (2003).

central motive. This responsibility to ensure justice is not only internally oriented, but it is an external responsibility as well. Specifically addressing humanitarian intervention, Henrik Syse, senior research fellow at the International Peace Research Institute in Oslo, argued that moral responsibility in the international arena, through such actions as humanitarian intervention, is Augustinian in character.[55] He reasoned that Augustine did not view justice only as the narrow defense of one's own interests, but rather he viewed it more broadly to include the punishment of wrongdoing and the nobler act of defending those that cannot defend themselves.[56] Additionally, James Turner Johnson argued that an idea of similar consequence could be found in Aquinas—specifically, in his prioritization of the just war principle of right authority over just cause.[57] The result of this prioritization is that the sovereign state is the authority with the responsibility to "serve the public good, the larger common good, and the natural order."[58] This propensity to affirm sovereign responsibility for justice, even outside of the sovereign borders of a nation-state, is characteristic of the classical view. Thus, adherents to classical views of natural law do not experience the dichotomy between international concern for human rights and state sovereignty because the same authority, God, is the foundation of both. In this regard, as long as the sovereign of the state adheres to his/her moral responsibilities, then the state's sovereignty should not be violated, and to do so would be unjust. However, if a state violates God-ordained natural law,

---

[55]Henrik Syse, "Augustine and Just War: Between Virtues and Duties," in *Ethics, Nationalism, and Just War: Medieval and Contemporary Perspectives*, ed. Henrik Syse and Gregory M. Reichberg (Washington, D.C.: Catholic University of America Press, 2007), 47-8.

[56]Ibid., 47.

[57]James Turner Johnson, "Thinking Morally About War in the Middle Ages and Today," in *Ethics, Nationalism, and Just War: Medieval and Contemporary Perspectives*, ed. Henrik Syse and Gregory M. Reichberg (Washington, D.C.: Catholic University of America Press, 2007), 6.

[58]Ibid.

other nations have the moral warrant, and even the responsibility, to intervene. However, this relationship changed in the modern era.

The Modern Views of Humanitarian Intervention

The modern view of natural law, which did not consider Divine authority, severed the moral link between sovereignty and intervention. On the modern view, the authority by which a state claimed sovereignty was either the consent of the people, or simply the sovereign's ability to rule, as will be shown below. The authority by which a state could claim the right to intervene in the affairs of another depended on which of two Enlightenment era views one took. Hensel divided the early-Enlightenment, anthropocentric view into two perspectives, the Hobbesian realist view, and the Lockean liberal view.[59] He also discussed thinkers from later in the Enlightenment era that rejected natural law, but he contends that they agree practically with the Hobbesian realists.[60] This section considers the views of humanitarian intervention from both the Hobbesian realist and the Lockean liberal perspectives.

For the Hobbesian realist, the principle source of motivation for action is the will of man influenced by personal or national interest.[61] Here, state sovereignty is justified by its ability to ensure survival of the state and act on the interests of the state internationally.[62] Similarly, regarding intervention, Hensel stated that the Hobbesian realist is "extremely reluctant to authorize intervention … except for reasons central to the vital national interests of the

---

[59]Hensel, "Anthropocentric Natural Law and Its Implications for International Relations and Armed Conflict."

[60]Hensel, "The Rejection of Natural Law and Its Implications for International Relations and Armed Conflict," 80.

[61]Hensel, "Anthropocentric Natural Law and Its Implications for International Relations and Armed Conflict," 34.

[62]Ibid., 38.

intervening power or powers."[63] As for the perspective of the Lockean liberal, which more closely resembles the ideals in modern democracies, the idea of state sovereignty was firmly grounded in the consent of the governed. In the words of John Locke, "Men being, as has been said, by nature, all free, equal, and independent, no one can be put out of this estate, and subjected to the political power of another, without his own consent."[64] Since Locke assumed self-evident inalienable rights as a natural feature of every man, states could then justify international intervention on this basis, if they desired. However, before a state could conduct an intervention, Lockean liberals generally required some form of request for assistance from the party experiencing aggression.[65] These two views of motivations to conduct humanitarian intervention, as well as the lack of authority that determines when action ought to be taken, create a different international order than that of the classical view.

For both modern views, the most important factor in the moral reasoning is that there is no inherent link between the authority by which one nation claims sovereignty, and the authority by which another nation claims a right to intervene. Therefore, when one state intervenes in the affairs of another, the first does so not only at the cost of the other's sovereignty, but also by subordinating the other's *justification* for its sovereignty. Since the basis by which one state claims sovereignty is not inherently binding on other states, when one state trumps another state's sovereignty, it is in effect claiming that the moral basis it has to intervene is of greater priority

---

[63]Ibid., 42.

[64]John Locke, "Two Treatises of Government," (1689), Chapter VIII, Section 95. Quoted from the Kindle edition.

[65]Hensel, "Anthropocentric Natural Law and Its Implications for International Relations and Armed Conflict," 51. Michael W. Doyle, *Ways of War and Peace: Realism, Liberalism, and Socialism* (New York: Norton, 1997), 221-2.

than the basis by which the other state claims sovereignty.[66] Without a unifying authority, such as God in the classical view, there is no objective means for prioritizing one nation's moral foundation over another's. For example, if a state is entrenched in a civil war and both sides request external assistance, by what basis is a state to judge between the moral rights of the two parties? One party has a claim what it views as a sovereign right, and the other has a moral claim to some form of abuse, oppression, or desire for greater freedoms in its governing institutions. Which of the two has the greater value? And on what basis would a state or coalition choose between the two, without prioritizing their own values, and intervening on behalf of the party whose values better match their own? Without a single value system that serves as an authority to make such value judgments, the decision appears arbitrary from the opposing view. This is true also in the case of the Lockean liberal's emphasis on a request for assistance. In this case, even if an oppressed people ask for help from other sovereign states, the moral calculus would remain unchanged. This is because there is no principle that provides moral warrant based on a request. So, even with a request, the decision to intervene remains morally arbitrary from the perspective of the intervened state.

This arbitrary ordering of values, perhaps, would not be so contentious if the international community consisted only of the state warranting intervention and the intervening state. However, international tensions increase when third-party nations understand the basis of their own sovereignty similarly to that of the intervened state. For these third-party states, the conclusion that their own sovereignty is arbitrarily subordinate to another's right to intervene is inescapable, and inherently threatening. This perhaps explains why sovereignty has been valued

---

[66]Hartley S. Spatt, "Faith, Force or Fellowship: The Future of Right Authority," in *Rethinking the Just War Tradition*, ed. Michael W. Brough, John W. Lango, and Harry Van der Linden (Albany: State University of New York Press, 2007), 291. Spatt presents a similar argument, but frames it in the context of a parent-child relationship, in which the intervening states "infantilizes, rather than restores" a state's sense of equality.

over human rights under the Westphalian international order. Because violating sovereignty without warrant is detrimental to the system. However, if an international authority existed that could determine when intervention is appropriate, this tension would be resolved. For modern thinkers, this authority cannot be God. Therefore, it must be a human institution of some form, such as the United Nations Security Council. Yet this only becomes necessary when the underlying values of states shift away from sovereignty and toward human rights in general, which is a product of postmodern morality.

The Postmodern View of Humanitarian Intervention: Giving Authority to International Institutions

Since the early 1990s, when the bipolar Cold War world ceased to exist, the postmodern moral views have gained influence in international relations. Professor of geopolitics at Virginia Tech, Gearóid Ó Tauthail, argued that globalization, informationalization and risk society have induced a postmodern geopolitical condition "where the boundaries that have traditionally delimited the geopolitical imagination are in crisis."[67] In addition to Professor Tauthail's list of postmodern influences, postmodern morality also presents such a challenge, because it devalues state borders. The postmodern moral emphasis on human rights and humanitarianism is easily regarded as positive because it appeals to common moral sensibilities regardless of whether one adheres to the modern or classical view of natural law. This is evident by the fact that states have claimed the prevention of human suffering as a motivation for intervention in the past. In fact, the United States claimed humanitarianism as its basis for intervention in the Spanish civil war in Cuba in 1898.[68] However, the postmodern view of morality entails motives that are antithetical to

---

[67]Gearóid Tuathail, "The Postmodern Geopolitical Condition: States, Statecraft, and Security at the Millennium," *Annals of the Association of American Geographers* 90, no. 1 (2000): 167.

[68]President McKinley's motivation for intervening in the Cuban revolutionary war was to "stop misery and death and protect American lives and property" among other things. See Allan

the borders and boundaries that define sovereignty in the traditional international system. To overcome the modern emphasis on sovereignty, the trend in the postmodern era is to institutionalize the authority to determine when sovereignty is subordinate to humanitarian concerns. The International Commission on Intervention and State Sovereignty (ICISS) Report of 2001 most clearly demonstrates this.

The commission's report, titled *The Responsibility to Protect*, argued "sovereign states have a responsibility to protect their own citizen from avoidable catastrophe – from mass murder and rape, from starvation – but that when they are unwilling or unable to do so, that responsibility must be borne by the broader community of states."[69] Included in the list of responsibilities laid out in the report is armed humanitarian intervention. As shown above, when a state or coalition chooses to violate the sovereignty of another state they implicitly, if not explicitly, prioritize their moral right to intervene over the other state's right to sovereignty. Yet, within the postmodern view there is no moral authority that gives such warrant. Therefore, a great deal of the report is an appeal to international bodies to assume such authorities—something they have been hesitant to do in the past. However, in 2005, partly because of the ICISS report, that changed.

The United Nations Secretary General Kofi Annan convened the "High-Level Panel on Threats, Challenges and Change" in 2004, and the resulting report stated,

> We endorse the emerging norm that there is a collective international
> responsibility to protect, exercisable by the Security Council authorizing military
> intervention as a last resort, in the event of genocide and other large-scale killing,

---

Reed Millett and Peter Maslowski, *For the Common Defense: A Military History of the United States of America* (New York: Free Press, 1984), 286. See also, Walter McDougall, *The Constitutional History of U.S. Foreign Policy: 222 Years of Tension in the Twilight Zone* (Philadelphia, PA: Foreign Policy Research Institute, 2010), 20.

[69]International Commission on Intervention and State Sovereignty, *The Responsibility to Protect*, VIII.

ethic cleansing or serious violations of international humanitarian law which sovereign Governments have proved powerless or unwilling to prevent.[70]

The following year, the United Nations World Summit adopted the language in the ICISS Report and stated that the UN is "prepared to take collective action, in a timely and decisive manner, through the Security Council, in accordance with the Charter, including Chapter VII [on the use of force], on a case-by-case basis."[71] In 2006 the UN Security Council reaffirmed this statement via Resolution 1674.[72] By explicitly assuming the authority to authorize humanitarian intervention, the UN has begun to fill the authority vacuum inherent in the postmodern moral perspective.[73] Although this has advanced the normalizing of the principles of responsibility to protect, there are still limitations inherent in the Security Council's processes that restrict its ability to act. In response to this fact, some have proposed creating an institution for the specific purpose of adjudicating when humanitarian intervention is appropriate.[74] In this on-going dialogue, the process of giving authority to international institutions is likely to continue as long as postmodern moral values remain influential.

---

[70]United Nations High-level Panel on Threats Challenges and Change, *A More Secure World: Our Shared Responsibility: Report of the High-Level Panel on Threats, Challenges, and Change* (New York: United Nations Dept. of Public Information, 2004), 57.

[71]United Nations General Assembly Sixtieth Session, *2005 World Summit Outcome* (New York: United Nations, 2005), 31.

[72]United Nations Securty Council, *Resolution 1674* (2006), 2.

[73]The arguments for increasing the authority of the United Nations are voluminous. See Spatt, "Faith, Force or Fellowship: The Future of Right Authority." See also Rice and Loomis, "The Evolution of Humanitarian Intervention and the Responsibility to Protect."

[74]Mohammed Ayoob, "Humanitarian Intervention and International Society," *Global Governance* 7, no. 3 (2001). Gillian Brock, "Humanitarian Intervention: Closing the Gap between Theory and Practice," *Journal of Applied Philosophy* 23, no. 3 (2006). John J. Davenport, "Just War Theory, Humanitarian Intervention, and the Need for a Democratic Federation," *Journal of Religious Ethics* 39, no. 3 (2011).

To summarize, just war originated with the view that states were accountable to God's authority and other states could conduct humanitarian interventions to maintain God-ordained justice in the international system. When the just war tradition was systematized to create the international order that exists today, the moral link between international concern for human rights and state sovereignty was severed and sovereignty was emphasized. However, along with postmodern morality came an emphasis on humanitarian concerns, and in accordance with the postmodern antipathy toward power boundaries, these concerns have taken priority over state sovereignty. But the system as devised in the modern era, lacked the authority to determine when humanitarian intervention is warranted, until recently. But the extant international bodies lack the process to be efficient in deciding and acting, so there is a continuing effort to create such an authority. However, there is still the question of the means to respond. This highlights another moral dimension of the discussion. Determining who should bear the risk of humanitarian intervention is also a moral question. And even if an institution is created that retains the authority to prioritize humanitarian concerns of a state's sovereignty, the question of means remains.

POSTMODERN MEANS: UNMANNED WARFARE

Samuel Huntington, the highly respected Harvard political scientist, writing about the U.S. intervention in Somalia, got to the heart of the issue of means in humanitarian intervention, "It is morally unjustifiable and politically indefensible that members of the Armed Forces should be killed to prevent Somalis from killing one another."[75] Even if the UN Security Council, or other international body has garnered the authority to authorize a humanitarian intervention, the question of means must be addressed. Currently, other individual nations or coalitions must bear the burden of supplying forces. While there is clear moral warrant for requiring military members

---

[75]Huntington, "New Contingencies, Old Roles," 10.

to assume risk on behalf of their own state and its politics—such is the reason for their existence—it is unclear what the moral basis would be for requiring individuals to assume risk for other states and their citizens, especially if the demand is from an international organization. Martin Cook, professor of military ethics at the Naval War College, phrased the issue succinctly "At its root, it goes to the implicit moral contract between the nation and its soldiers."[76] Since there is no such contract or implicit understanding between the U.N. or other international body and the citizens of a given nation, risking military men and women is even less justifiable. Moreover, many nations lack the means to intervene even when they desire to do so, as in the case of the African Union in Sudan.[77] Additionally, those that have the means to conduct humanitarian interventions, often lack the will, as in the case of Rwanda in the 1990s. For such reasons, commentators often recommend generating a standing force that would conduct the actions when authorized by the appropriate international institution.[78] However, the question of who should fulfill such a requirement remains. As Huntington pointed out, requiring forces that are obligated to national defense is "politically indefensible." Michael Gross, professor of international relations at Haifa University in Israel, suggests that such a force would require volunteers.[79] But there is potentially a less risky solution.

---

[76]Martin L. Cook, *The Moral Warrior: Ethics and Service in the U.S. Military* (Albany, NY: State University of New York Press, 2004), 123.

[77]Jashobanta Pan, "African Union's Intervention in Sudan: Importance and Effectiveness," *Insight on Africa* 2, (2010).

[78]Walzer, *Just and Unjust Wars: A Moral Argument with Historical Illustrations*, xiii. James Pattison, "Whose Responsibility to Protect? The Duties of Humanitarian Intervention," *Journal of Military Ethics* 7, no. 4 (2008): 273. Rice and Loomis, "The Evolution of Humanitarian Intervention and the Responsibility to Protect," 89-90.

[79]Michael L. Gross, *Moral Dilemmas of Modern War: Torture, Assassination, and Blackmail in an Age of Asymmetric Conflict* (Cambridge: Cambridge University Press, 2010), 228.

Unmanned combat vehicles, or more colloquially, "drones," have advanced in both capability and utilization over the past decade.[80] Their use is rightly surrounded with debate that frequently uses moral language. It seems that no other system since nuclear weapons have sparked such great debate. Of course, nuclear weapons were only used once; drone use, on the other hand, is prevalent and growing rapidly. They serve great utility in assisting combatants on the battlefield. However, they can also serve to isolate combatants from the battlefield. The postmodern advent of risk-free warfare has created great debate on the justice of such means.

Many in the Western media argue that drones should be restricted or banned because of how they are used, specifically in targeted assassinations, or because the international implications of drone proliferation are either unknown or not understood.[81] Foreign policy analyst Adam Elkus associated these types of arguments with similar arguments made against older means of warfare such as crossbows and long-range bombers. He then countered that, since we do not consider these weapons objectionable now, we should not deny ourselves capabilities because of an "anachronistic view" of war.[82] Nevertheless, if the means of warfare can influence the decision to use force internationally, then that means warrants consideration in relation to the *jus ad bellum* principle of last resort. Additionally, they must also be considered from the *jus in bello* perspective. These assessments will determine if there are any moral or philosophical prohibitions for using drones in humanitarian intervention.

---

[80]The word "drones" used here signifies all unmanned combat vehicles regardless of the medium on which they operate.

[81]John Kaag and Sarah Kreps, "The Moral Hazard of Drones", nytimes.com http://opinionator.blogs.nytimes.com/2012/07/22/the-moral-hazard-of-drones/. Jeffrey Goldberg, "Drones: The Morality of War from the Sky" http://www.businessweek.com/articles/2012-10-11/drones-the-morality-of-war-from-the-sky (accessed 15 October 2012). This is an example of a contemporary argument against drones.

[82]Adam Elkus, "Death from Above: The West and the Rest", Small Wars Journal http://smallwarsjournal.com/jrnl/art/death-from-above (accessed 27 November 2012).

Drones and *Jus Ad Bellum*

The principles of *jus ad bellum* do not inherently reduce war; they only provide a means to evaluate the decisions made to go to war. Such decisions are judged to determine if the war is just or unjust. War conducted with drones, however, presents no obvious connection between drones as a means of warfare and six of the seven *jus ad bellum* principles. The principles of just cause, right authority, right intention, proportionality of ends, reasonable hope of success, and the aim of peace will apply to the decision to go to war regardless of the means selected, and the means bears little on that judgment. However, if drones can influence the political decision to utilize violence internationally *before* considering other feasible nonviolent options, then it is possible to declare the war unjust because the *jus ad bellum* principle of last resort was violated. Can drones have this kind of influence?

Regarding war, Clausewitz contended that, "no other human activity is so continuously or universally bound up with chance." [83] This leads to the conclusion that the decision to go to war is inextricably linked to an assessment of risk. To answer the question of drone influence on go-to-war-decisions, it helps to understand if drone warfare is, in fact, inherently less risky than other nonviolent options. If so, then utilizing them before these other means may violate the just war principle of last resort. Because, if a means of war can greatly reduce the risk associated with its use, then it is a plausible conclusion that states may more readily pursue political goals using such means. [84] To explore the relationship between drones and risk decisions, two questions are appropriate. The first is how much do drones reduce the risks involved in warfare? For this

---

[83] Clausewitz, *On War*, 85.

[84] There is a conspicuous paucity of military professional writing concerning the influence of drones on risk analysis in use-of-force decision-making. Writers generally assume that the reduction in risk to force justifies expansion of drone utilization, or they focus on the moral and legal implications of particular drone missions.

question, it is helpful to categorize two types of risk that decision-makers must consider when going to war—risk to force and political risk.[85] The second question gets to the heart of the last resort principle—if there is a risk reduction, is it so great that political leaders will default to the drone option *before* exploring other viable options? Briefly exploring these two questions will clarify the justice of drones as a means of war, particularly in reference to the *jus ad bellum* principle of last resort.

There can be little doubt that drones present a substantial reduction in risk to the lives of their operators. When it is possible for combatants to transition from home to combat without assuming any more risk than what the drive to work demands, then that element of the nation's combat force is assuming no more risk than the nation's work force. The risk at this point is as low as it can possibly be. However, there are two aspects that are worthy of some consideration. First, for the current technology of drones, there are always forces forward deployed with the drones that must launch and recover the vehicles. However, while these forces are not operating at home, it is not necessary that they be so near the battle space as to assume great risk. Secondly, there may be some other more long-term psychological risks involved in engaging in this type of warfare for the home operators. Air Force surgeon Colonel Hernando Ortega described the psychological effects of "telewarfare" as something akin to an "existential conflict," which is different from post-traumatic stress disorder (PTSD), and research into the long-term effects are

---

[85]Risk to mission is not considered in this research because the risk to mission assessment requires considering drone capabilities in relation to a specific mission, which, ultimately, is a practical question, not a moral one. If the fielded drone technology is viable for the given mission then the following risk to force and political risk assessments are applicable. If the technology is not a viable option practically, then it obviously will not influence political decisions. It is beyond the scope of this research to determine if the currently fielded technology is practically viable for any specific mission. Therefore, when considering both risk to force and political risk assessments, it is assumed that the drone technology is capable of accomplishing the mission under consideration.

just beginning.[86] Yet, for any new disorders to present so great a risk to force as to reduce the political likelihood of drone use, they would need to be substantial—more substantial than PTSD. They are not likely to be. Also, there are existing ways of coping with and managing combat stress disorders. So, while there may be other unforeseen long-term psychological risks to force associated with drone warfare, there are structures in place to handle such issues. Therefore, since drones greatly reduce the risk to their operators and there is low probability that any long-term psychological factors will influence political decision, it is likely that drones will influence a political risk to force calculus.

Also, there is always political risk associated with the international use of force. It can be considered in two categories, domestic political risk and international political risk, because the views of the populace can, and often do, vary from that of the international community. For instance, the Pew Research Center conducted a survey in 2012 of twenty countries on the topic of U.S. foreign policy. The results regarding U.S. drone strikes showed that a majority of people in each country surveyed disapproved—in many countries, they overwhelmingly disapproved. However, Americans approved 62 percent to 28 percent.[87] It is important not to infer from the survey that there is international opposition to drones in general; rather the opposition is to drone *strikes*. The motivations for such opposition can range from pacifist views to general distrust of American foreign policy. Yet, people may oppose drone strikes because they are a relatively new addition to warfare and currently ubiquitous in the media. Thus, as the novelty wanes, it is possible that so will the press coverage as well as the opposition. Then political leaders will

---

[86]"Combat Stress in Remotely Piloted/Uas Operations," in *Combat Stress in Remotely Piloted/UAS Operations* (VA: The Brookings Institute, 2012), 31 and 51.

[87]"Global Opinion of Obama Slips, International Policies Faulted", Pew Research Center http://www.pewglobal.org/2012/06/13/global-opinion-of-obama-slips-international-policies-faulted/ (accessed 27 November 2012).

realize the full influence of drones on political risk calculations, at least for those missions and operations that generate media attention, because there is an inherent quality in drone warfare that reduces its political risk. New York Times reporter, David Sanger, citing U.S. national security aides, noted that the appeal of drones is in their "precision, economy and *deniability*."[88] It is this deniability that, without doubt, will influence political use of force decisions. Some may argue that deniability in the conduct of operations is not novel to drone warfare, because it has always been a defining characteristic of special operations forces (SOF). However, there is definite risk to force associated with the use of SOF, and there is not with drones. This makes drones politically less risky. Thus, while the full effects of drones on political risk is not yet known, there is reason to believe that they will reduce the political risks associated with decisions to use force internationally, if for no other reason than that they are deniable.

Given the conclusions that drones reduce political risk and risk to force, the question becomes how does this overall reduction in risk effect "last resort" considerations. Specifically, does the reduced risk mean that political leaders *will* use force instead of other viable means? To assert such a logical certainty would be to commit the slippery slope fallacy. Nothing in the assessment above can lead to the certain conclusion that, because drones reduce risk, their use will always be unjust. However, the assessment does point to the probability of political actors using drones to resolve conflicts that would be too risky or not viable for manned operations, where otherwise such action would not be taken.

In summary, there is nothing inherent in drone use that violates the *jus ad bellum* principle of last resort, which leads to the conclusion that such judgments will not prevent drone use as a means to achieve postmodern ends. However, the decreased risk drone warfare provides

---

[88]David E. Sanger, *Confront and Conceal: Obama's Secret Wars and Surprising Use of American Power* (New York: Crown Publishers, 2012), 246. Emphasis added.

may provide impetus for leaders to use force more frequently than otherwise, particularly for the missions and operations for which it is well suited. But, are such a means a just way to fight?

Drones and *Jus In Bello*

The question of the just use of unmanned combat vehicles involves a *jus in bello* assessment. Two of the fundamental concepts that serve as the foundation of the *jus in bello* principles are the moral equivalency of combatants and protected status of civilians. Yale University professor of law and humanities, Dr. Paul Kahn said, "The fundamental moral fact about war is that the innocent are appropriate targets of physical violence—not, of course, all of the morally innocent. The morality of the battlefield distinguishes not between the innocent and the guilty, but between the combatant and the noncombatant."[89] He argued that riskless warfare, an inherent characteristic of drone operations, "pushes up against the limits of the traditional moral justification of combat."[90] This, perhaps, is evident in the great quantity of media arguments against drone use. It also points to a general perception of ignobility with killing at a distance, even if the pure philosophical reasoning may not be clear.[91] This section will clarify the philosophical reasoning behind this sense of ignobility in risk-free warfare. When using such means in combat, two philosophical problems arise—the self-defense justification for killing and the moral restraint that prevents killing.

The self-defense justification for killing is founded in the moral equivalency of combatants. This idea provides the basis on which a combatant on either side may kill an enemy

---

[89]Paul W. Kahn, "The Paradox of Riskless Warfare," *Philosophy and Public Policy Quarterly* 22, no. 3 (2002): 2.

[90]Ibid.

[91]B. J. Strawser, "Moral Predators: The Duty to Employ Uninhabited Aerial Vehicles," *Journal of Military Ethics* 9, no. 4 (2010): 357. Strawser admits in his argument for the obligation to use drones that something does appear to be "ignoble or dishonorable" with distant warfare. He says that this felling in itself does not amount to an argument against drones.

combatant in self-defense, based solely on the existential threat that the enemy poses. Dr. Kahn pointed out the paradox that ensues when drones are used as a sole means in war,

> If the fundamental principle of the morality of warfare is a right to exercise self-defense within the conditions of mutual imposition of risk, then the emergence of asymmetrical warfare represents a deep challenge. A regime capable of targeting and destroying others with the push of a button, with no human intervention but only the operation of the ultimate high tech weapon, propels us well beyond the ethics of warfare. Such a deployment of force might be morally justified—it might be used to promote morally appropriate ends—but we cannot appeal to the morality of warfare to justify this mode of combat.[92]

In this sense, combatants are only combatants if they stand in a relationship of mutual risk, meaning that one can only be considered a combatant if he/she poses a risk. Thus, if someone does not pose a risk to the lives of others, then that individual is not a combatant and therefore, immune from attack. Kahn concluded that this paradox challenges the *jus in bello* principle of discrimination stating, "if we cannot adequately discriminate between the morally guilty and the innocent, we may not be able to use force at all."[93] Currently, this paradox is overcome by the fact that, while the drone operator may not be at risk, some combatants from his/her nation are. And it is the risk assumed by those combatants that warrants killing an enemy. However, with exclusive drone use, and therefore, risk-free warfare, the foundation of the *jus in bello* moral justification for killing in war becomes less about the restrictive idea of *self-defense*, and more about *defense* in general.

This shift from self-defense to defense in general means that justifying the act of killing is closer to that of policing than of warfare.[94] Consider the following example. A police officer is charged with protecting a population and upholding law. If an officer, then, happens upon an

---

[92]Kahn, "The Paradox of Riskless Warfare," 3.

[93]Ibid., 5.

[94]Ibid. Dr. Kahn stresses this idea throughout his article.

individual with a gun pointed at another, the officer is morally responsible for the protection of the individual, and based on the aggressor's moral guilt, has moral warrant to kill. Conversely, if a soldier in a warzone happens upon two civilians in the same situation, that soldier, while likely feeling the need to act, lacks the moral warrant to kill the aggressor, because his/her justification for killing is not based on moral guilt or innocence. Rather, it is based on combatant status, which the civilian aggressor lacks in the scenario. When the moral warrant for killing is more about general defense than self-defense, as is the case with risk-free warfare, the act of killing is more similar to policing than warfare.

This shift of moral warrant creates confusion that drives the justification for killing away from the rules of regular warfare based on combatant status, and toward the rules of irregular warfare based on guilt. If combatants have a responsibility and moral warrant to kill for defense in general, they must do so based on laws that delineate guilt from innocence, as is the case for police officers. If no such laws exist or are not expressed clearly to soldiers, then they are liable to kill without warrant or not kill when they ought. This creates the situation where they are at risk of bearing moral guilt for not killing, as well as for killing unjustly, while the factors that influence such decisions have greatly increased. This is the result of the shift to defense in general as the moral justification for killing in combat, which is the required justification for risk-free drone warfare. But the responsibilities, restrictions, and decisions of the drone operators are not the only changes that result from drone use.

Drones also change the moral calculus of the enemy populace in which they are deployed. The introduction of drones into the battlefield environment removes the moral component of decisions made by the opposition whether they are combatants or not.[95] One of the

---

[95]Recall Kahn's argument presented above that in risk-free warfare, combatant status is questionable.

deterrents to killing in combat, even justifiable killing is the fact that the death of another human beings is involved. There are numerous cases in history when combatants had both the warrant and the means to kill an enemy combatant but did not.[96] Drones remove that deterrent completely for the opposition, because they have no moral restraint from attacking the technology as they would for attacking another human being. In other words, they have no moral restrictions to prevent them from destroying the technology by any means available. Also, since no actual killing is involved, they have no need to separate combatants from noncombatants. This is because when the moral responsibility of killing is gone, all have a responsibility to defend the community from outside aggression. Conversely, the state that utilizes the drones has no moral warrant to respond if someone does attack its technology, since it is not morally justifiable to kill only in defense of offensive technology, even if the war is just. However, this does not mean that all killing with drone technology is morally unjustifiable, because defense is a valid purpose for killing, but not necessarily defense of technology. If someone is declared morally guilty by killing or threatening to kill someone whom a drone operator is tasked to protect, then killing with drones is justifiable. So what does this mean for the use of drones for postmodern ends?

Drones and Postmodern Ends

The question of the moral viability of such a weapon system to conduct humanitarian intervention remains. Michael Walzer said "humanitarian intervention comes much closer than any other kind of intervention to what we commonly regard, in domestic society, as law enforcement and police work."[97] Also, the goal of humanitarian intervention is to protect an existentially threatened people, and the moral warrant for killing during such operations—moral

---

[96]Michael Walzer discusses several accounts of such events. See the section titled "The Status of Individuals" in Walzer, *Just and Unjust Wars: A Moral Argument with Historical Illustrations*, 138-43.

[97]Ibid., 106.

guilt—is the same justification required to kill using risk-free drone technology. In fact, Dr. Kahn said of the risk relationship between fighting groups that, "a perfect technology of justice would achieve a perfect asymmetry: the morally guilty should suffer all the risk and all the injury."[98] Such a perfect asymmetry between the morally guilty and the instrument of justice is achieved in the currently fielded drone technology.

There are other practical considerations as well. There is the possibility that the announced presence of drones conducting a humanitarian protection mission within a specific state could serve as a deterrent, since the aggressive actors may perceive that they have been placed in a virtual panopticon. There is also the necessary regard for collateral damage. For situations in which weapons employment is warranted, the currently fielded weapons technology may lack the precision necessary to prevent collateral damage and the killing of those warranting protection. Although, some argue that they should bear the greater share of risk in such operations, and political actors may assume some risk in this regard as the existence of the threatened is likely already in jeopardy due to belligerent parties.[99]

In summary, from a *jus ad bellum* view, there is nothing inherent in drones that would render all use of force decisions, in which such means were used, as unjust. Also, the justification for killing with drones in the *jus in bello* assessment demonstrates that such killing requires justification similar to policing operations, which is what humanitarian intervention most resembles. This conclusion combined with the fact that there is nothing inherent in drone warfare that violates the *jus ad bellum* principle of last resort, means that drones present a morally viable

---

[98]Kahn, "The Paradox of Riskless Warfare," 4.

[99]Gerhard Overland, "High-Fliers: Who Should Bear the Risk of Humanitarian Intervention?," in *New Wars and New Soldiers: Military Ethics in the Contemporary World*, ed. Paolo Tripodi and Jessica Wolfendale (Burlington, VT: Ashgate, 2011).

option for decision makers as a means to conduct humanitarian intervention. They are, in fact, so well suited for such a mission, that it may even be morally irresponsible not to consider them.[100]

CONCLUSION

Having explored postmodern morality and the progression of moral thought that preceded it, and the influence of such moral reasoning on international ends, as well as the philosophical and moral viability of drones to achieve such ends, it is beneficial to synthesize this information to try to discern what these factors portend for the future. But first, a brief review is appropriate.

Three views of morality, as reflected in the progress of Western thought, have been presented. God and his directives are the foundation of the classical view, in which all of mankind as well as sovereign states are morally accountable to his divine law. This is the view on which the just war tradition was founded. During this period both state sovereignty and human rights depended on the laws of God, and these laws provided a means of judging their relative values.

Then in the modern era, man and reason became the foundation of morality, with the rejection of a creator God, and exaltation of the scientific method and observation as the principle source of knowledge. During this era, philosophers and jurists from the early modern era founded the international system by systematizing the just war tradition apart from its historical foundation—God. When that source was rejected, there was an emphasis on the primacy of national sovereignty, since there was no longer a moral warrant that required states to intervene in other states' affairs for the sake of international justice. Political actions alone defined war and international conflict with little to no necessity for the idea of moral justice. Finally, the

---

[100]Strawser, "Moral Predators: The Duty to Employ Uninhabited Aerial Vehicles," 343-4. Strawser argues for what he calls the principle of unnecessary risk, which states that no one ought to be ordered to assume more risk than is required to accomplish a task. From here he reasons that if there is a means of accomplishing the task with lesser risk, leaders have a moral obligation to employ such a means.

postmodern view developed in contrast to modernity and contends that all knowledge, to include moral knowledge, is relative to the individual and that attempts to require one's own moral code of others is motivated by a desire to obtain power. Postmodern thinkers desire conversely to empower the marginalized within society, as well as devalue the boundaries that define power structures. The friction between sovereignty and humanitarian intervention has risen as a concomitant of postmodern morality.

After World War II humanitarian concerns came to the fore in international affairs with the signing of the United Nations Declaration on Human Rights, and over the decades since humanitarian concerns have advanced internationally. This is attributable to the postmodern exaltation of the oppressed and their narrative, as well as antipathy for the boundaries that define power. The international acceptance of responsibility to protect is the most obvious result. However, the conflict of international norms that results from stressing both state sovereignty in international law as well as the responsibility to protect as an international ethic requires that a qualified international body have the responsibility of authorizing intervention. The U.N. General Assembly offered this authority to the U.N. Security Council, which accepted it. But the process by which humanitarian intervention must be approved in the Security Council is inefficient and does not meet the intent of the intervention ethic. Therefore the drive to institutionalize the ethic in a more efficient body continues in literature on the topic.

Additionally, while most states agree to the concept of responsibility to protect in principle, few have the capability to act or to intervene and prevent any pending moral atrocity. However, the postmodern means of war—unmanned combat vehicles—are well suited for such tasks. They can, perhaps, deter atrocities with an overt presence, and take action against identified aggressors if warranted. Because of their risk-free nature, they create a near perfect asymmetry of risk between the morally guilty and instruments of justice, so that national militaries are not required to assume any risk in taking action. This deterrence and asymmetry of risk make drones a logical option for humanitarian intervention.

It is possible given the assessment above to anticipate what these trends mean for the future of international relations. The postmodern moral influence on international relations, combined with the current and developing context of unmanned warfare, portend a shift in the international system toward an international police organization with the authority and means to execute police functions within otherwise sovereign states. Paradoxically, the very idea of postmodernism as a moral and philosophical position originated from a motivation to deconstruct power structures. Yet, when international actors make these postmodern ideas practical and act on them, the result forebodes a greater structure of international authority. The power and authority is transferred from the state to an international body, it is not dispersed. This conclusion can stand, as presented, only as long as postmodern morals continue to influence international relations. This report has also highlighted some other areas worthy of further research.

Much of the writing on drone warfare assumes that this technology will continue to proliferate to perform a wide variety of combat functions because such technology greatly reduces risk for combatants. Thus, there is a noticeable paucity of theoretical analysis on the influence of drones on use of force decision-making. How important is the asymmetry of risk in drone warfare in making use of force decisions? Does it create a willingness in leaders to resort to the use of force before other potential options? Conversely, from the perspective of the enemy, is there a limit to drone development and advancement beyond which other states will be obligated to take action? If so, will destroying the technology be adequate or will more drastic measures to do harm to the agent be required? The answers to such questions are important to understand if drones are in fact proliferating to the point in which nations bear little or no risk when using force internationally.

Because of the synthesis of the postmodern international influences, as well the trends they presage, this report adds to the growing dialogue regarding both responsibility to protect and the morality of drone warfare. These international ideas and actions that portend an international body with the authority and means to conduct police-style operations are important to understand given the other challenges and changes in the current international order. International terrorism, the growing influence of non-governmental agencies, U.N. reform, and the management of "ungoverned spaces" are some examples of pressures in the international arena that either increase authority of international institutions, decrease the relevance of international borders, or that shift authority from the state to international bodies. Postmodern morals, ends, and means can be added to that list.

BIBLIOGRAPHY

Aquinas, Thomas. *Summa Theologica*, 1274.

Ayoob, Mohammed. "Humanitarian Intervention and International Society." *Global Governance* 7, no. 3 (2001): 225-230.

Best, Geoffrey. *War and Law since 1945*. Oxford: Oxford University Press, 1994.

Brock, Gillian. "Humanitarian Intervention: Closing the Gap between Theory and Practice." *Journal of Applied Philosophy* 23, no. 3 (2006): 277-291.

Charter of the United Nations and Statute of the International Court of Justice. San Francisco, 1945.

Clausewitz, Carl von. *On War*. Translated by Michael Howard and Peter Paret. Princeton, NJ: Princeton University Press, 1976.

"Combat Stress in Remotely Piloted/Uas Operations." In *Combat Stress in Remotely Piloted/UAS Operations*. VA: The Brookings Institute, 2012.

Cook, Martin L. *The Moral Warrior: Ethics and Service in the U.S. Military*. Albany, NY: State University of New York Press, 2004.

Davenport, John J. "Just War Theory, Humanitarian Intervention, and the Need for a Democratic Federation." *Journal of Religious Ethics* 39, no. 3 (2011): 493-555.

Douzinas, C. "Postmodern Just Wars and the New World Order." *JOURNAL OF HUMAN RIGHTS* 5, no. 3 (2006): 355-375.

Doyle, Michael W. *Ways of War and Peace: Realism, Liberalism, and Socialism*. New York: Norton, 1997.

Elkus, Adam. "Death from Above: The West and the Rest". Small Wars Journal http://smallwarsjournal.com/jrnl/art/death-from-above (accessed 27 November 2012).

Fisher, David. *Morality and War: Can War Be Just in the Twenty-First Century?* Oxford; New York: Oxford University Press, 2011.

"Global Opinion of Obama Slips, International Policies Faulted". Pew Research Center http://www.pewglobal.org/2012/06/13/global-opinion-of-obama-slips-international-policies-faulted/ (accessed 27 November 2012).

Goldberg, Jeffrey. "Drones: The Morality of War from the Sky" http://www.businessweek.com/articles/2012-10-11/drones-the-morality-of-war-from-the-sky (accessed 15 October 2012).

Gray, Chris Hables. *Postmodern War: The New Politics of Conflict*. New York: Guilford Press, 1997.

Gray, Phillip Wesley. *'That Truth That Lives Unchangeably': The Role of Ontology in the Just War Tradition*. College Station, TX: Texas A&M University, 2007. http://hdl.handle.net/1969.1/4715.

Gross, Michael L. *Moral Dilemmas of Modern War: Torture, Assassination, and Blackmail in an Age of Asymmetric Conflict*. Cambridge: Cambridge University Press, 2010.

Grotius, Hugo. *De Jure Belli Ac Pacis Libre Tres*. Translated by Francis W. Kelsey. Vol. 2 Classics of International Law, Edited by James B. Scott. New York: Oceana Publications, 1964.

Hensel, Howard M. "Theocentric Natural Law and the Norms of the Global Community." In *Sovereignty and the Global Community: The Quest for Order in the International System*, edited by Howard M. Hensel, 1-53. Aldershot, Hants, England: Ashgate, 2004.

_____. "Anthropocentric Natural Law and Its Implications for International Relations and Armed Conflict." In *The Legitimate Use of Military Force: The Just War Tradition and the Customary Law of Armed Conflict*, edited by Howard M. Hensel, 29-62. Aldershot, England: Ashgate, 2008.

_____. "The Rejection of Natural Law and Its Implications for International Relations and Armed Conflict." In *The Legitimate Use of Military Force: The Just War Tradition and the Customary Law of Armed Conflict*, edited by Howard M. Hensel, 63-96. Aldershot, England: Ashgate, 2008.

_____. "Theocentric Natural Law and Just War Doctrine." In *The Legitimate Use of Military Force: The Just War Tradition and the Customary Law of Armed Conflict*, edited by Howard M. Hensel, 5-27. Aldershot, England: Ashgate, 2008.

Hobbes, Thomas. *Leviathan*. 1651.

Huntington, Samuel P. "New Contingencies, Old Roles." *Joint Forces Quarterly*, no. 34 (2003): 6.

Ilcan, Suzan. "From Modernity to Postmodernity." In *Postmodernism and the Ethical Subject*, edited by Barbara Gabriel and Suzan Ilcan Montreal, QC, CAN: McGill-Queen's University Press, 2004.

International Commission on Intervention and State Sovereignty. *The Responsibility to Protect*. Ottawa: International development research centre, 2001.

Johnson, James Turner. "Thinking Morally About War in the Middle Ages and Today." In *Ethics, Nationalism, and Just War: Medieval and Contemporary Perspectives*, edited by Henrik Syse and Gregory M. Reichberg. Washington, D.C.: Catholic University of America Press, 2007.

_____. *Ethics and the Use of Force*. Burlington, VT: Ashgate, 2011.

Kaag, John, and Sarah Kreps. "The Moral Hazard of Drones". nytimes.com http://opinionator.blogs.nytimes.com/2012/07/22/the-moral-hazard-of-drones/.

Kahn, Paul W. "The Paradox of Riskless Warfare." *Philosophy and Public Policy Quarterly* 22, no. 3 (2002): 5.

Lefkowitz, David. "On a Duty of Humanitarian Intervention." In *New Wars and New Soldiers: Military Ethics in the Contemporary World*, edited by Paolo Tripodi and Jessica Wolfendale, 87-101. Farnham Surrey, UK: Ashgate, 2011.

Locke, John. *Two Treatises of Government.* 1689.

Lyotard, Jean-Francois. *The Postmodern Condition: A Report on Knowledge.* Minneapolis: University of Minnesota Press, 1984.

McDougall, Walter. *The Constitutional History of U.S. Foreign Policy: 222 Years of Tension in the Twilight Zone.* Philadelphia, PA: Foreign Policy Research Institute, 2010.

Mill, John Stuart. *A Few Words on Non-Intervention.* Edited by Libertarian Alliance. London: Libertarian Alliance, 1859.

Millett, Allan Reed, and Peter Maslowski. *For the Common Defense: A Military History of the United States of America.* New York: Free Press, 1984.

Moskos, Charles C., and James Burk. "The Postmodern Military." In *The Military in New Times*, edited by James Burk, 141-180. Boulder, CO: Westview Press, 1994.

Overland, Gerhard. "High-Fliers: Who Should Bear the Risk of Humanitarian Intervention?" In *New Wars and New Soldiers: Military Ethics in the Contemporary World*, edited by Paolo Tripodi and Jessica Wolfendale, 69-86. Burlington, VT: Ashgate, 2011.

Pan, Jashobanta. "African Union's Intervention in Sudan: Importance and Effectiveness." *Insight on Africa* 2, (2010): 15.

Pattison, James. "Whose Responsibility to Protect? The Duties of Humanitarian Intervention." *Journal of Military Ethics* 7, no. 4 (2008): 22.

Pearcey, Nancy. *Saving Leonardo: A Call to Resist the Secular Assault on Mind, Morals, & Meaning.* Nashville, TN: B&H Publishing, 2010.

Rice, Susan E., and Andrew J. Loomis. "The Evolution of Humanitarian Intervention and the Responsibility to Protect." In *Beyond Preemption: Force and Legitimacy in a Changing World*, edited by Ivo H. Daalder, 59-95. Washington, D.C.: Brookings Institution Press, 2007.

Robinson, Paul. *Just War in Comparative Perspective.* Aldershot, Hampshire, England: Ashgate, 2003.

Sanger, David E. *Confront and Conceal: Obama's Secret Wars and Surprising Use of American Power.* New York: Crown Publishers, 2012.

45

Schaeffer, Francis. *How Should We Then Live? (L'abri 50th Anniversary Edition): The Rise and Decline of Western Thought and Culture*. Wheaton, IL: Crossway Books, 2005.

Spatt, Hartley S. "Faith, Force or Fellowship: The Future of Right Authority." In *Rethinking the Just War Tradition*, edited by Michael W. Brough, John W. Lango and Harry Van der Linden, 205-222. Albany: State University of New York Press, 2007.

Strawser, B. J. "Moral Predators: The Duty to Employ Uninhabited Aerial Vehicles." *Journal of Military Ethics* 9, no. 4 (2010): 27.

Stumpf, Christoph A. *The Grotian Theology of International Law: Hugo Grotius and the Moral Foundations of International Relations*. Vol. 44 Religion and Society, Edited by Gustavo Benavides and Kocku von Stuckrad. Berlin: Walter de Gruyter, 2006.

Syse, Henrik. "Augustine and Just War: Between Virtues and Duties." In *Ethics, Nationalism, and Just War: Medieval and Contemporary Perspectives*, edited by Henrik Syse and Gregory M. Reichberg, 36-50. Washington, D.C.: Catholic University of America Press, 2007.

Tuathail, Gearóid. "The Postmodern Geopolitical Condition: States, Statecraft, and Security at the Millennium." *Annals of the Association of American Geographers* 90, no. 1 (2000): 166-178.

United Nations General Assembly Sixtieth Session. *2005 World Summit Outcome*. New York: United Nations, 2005.

United Nations High-level Panel on Threats Challenges and Change. *A More Secure World: Our Shared Responsibility: Report of the High-Level Panel on Threats, Challenges, and Change*. New York: United Nations Dept. of Public Information, 2004.

United Nations Securty Council. *Resolution 1674*. 2006.

Vreeland, Hamilton. *Hugo Grotius, the Father of the Modern Science of International Law*. New York: Oxford University Press, American Branch, 1917.

Walzer, Michael. *Just and Unjust Wars: A Moral Argument with Historical Illustrations*. New York: Basic Books, 1977.

Wells, David F. *God in the Wasteland: The Reality of Truth in a World of Fading Dreams*. Grand Rapids, MI: W.B. Eerdmans, 1994.

Yenne, Bill. *Attack of the Drones: A History of Unmanned Aerial Combat*. St. Paul, MN: MBI Pub. Co., 2004.